TAKAI Armstead

Reach for the Stars.

Leslie M.
2018

Mommy, Do You Work Tonight?

Copyright © 2017 by Leslie T. Marshall

No part of this publication may be produced, stored in a retrieval system or transmitted by any way means, electrical, mechanical, photocopy, recording or otherwise without proper permission of author except as provided by USA copyright law.

Scripture quotations, unless otherwise indicated, are takes from The Holy Bible, King James Version, Cambridge, 1769. Used by permission. All rights reserved.

The opinions expressed by the author are not necessarily those of Fountain of Life Publisher's House.

Published by Fountain of Life Publisher's House
P. O. Box 922612, Norcross, Georgia, 30010 Phone: 404.936.3989

Fountain of Life Publisher's House is committed to excellence in the publishing industry. The company reflects the philosophy established by the founders based on Psalms 68:11, "The Lord gave the word and great was those of the company of those who published it."

Cover Design & Illustrated by: Niaren Binford
Editor: Phyllis R Brown and Wednesday I. Webb

ISBN: 978-1537579382
January 2017

Mommy Do You Work Tonight?

By

Leslie T. Marshall

Illustrations by

Niaren Binford

Every morning Denzel woke up with one question on his mind. Before he would say his prayers, or brush his teeth, he had to know, "Mommy, do you work tonight?"

Denzel was six years old and his baby sister Diamond was two years old. They lived with their Mom and Great Grandmother, Joyce. "Granny," is what they called her. She took great care of them while their mom worked late in the evening hours, from 7pm-7am; twelve long hours from night to the morning.

When Mommy arrived home in the morning, she was usually very sleepy. She could not go straight to bed because she had to help the children, get dressed, eat a quick breakfast; and drop them off to school. While they were in school mommy would clean up, prepare dinner, and then get some sleep. In a few hours, she would have to pick the children up from school, go over homework, and finally get herself ready for work.

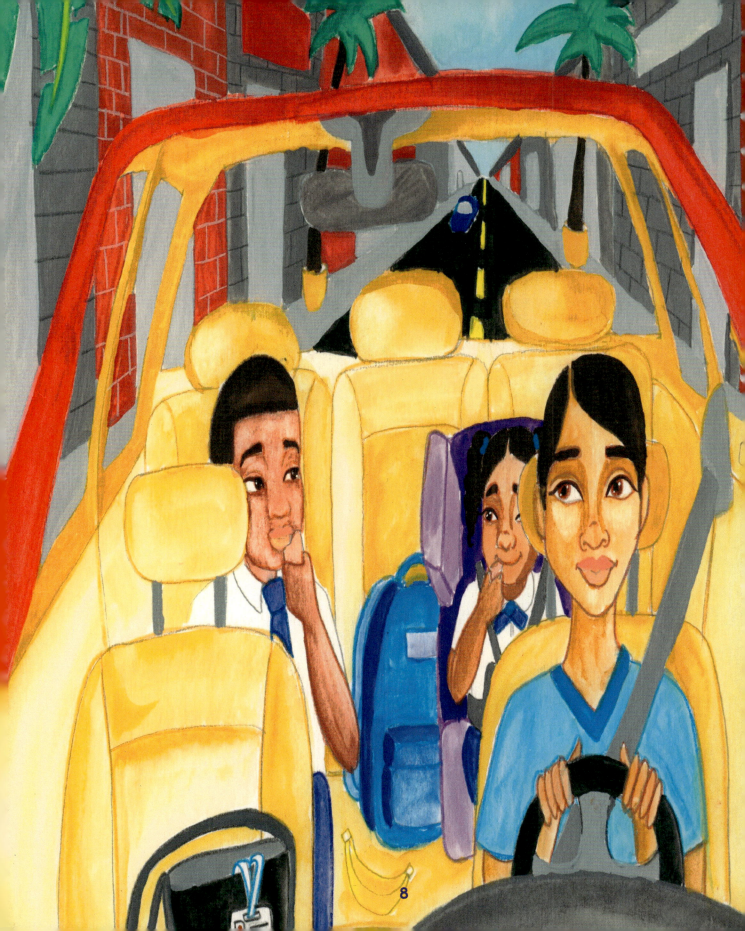

Boy, did they keep Granny busy! Denzel loved to read books, and pour his own juice; sometimes at the same time. He was the best at making hot cocoa and promised not to make a mess this time. He was a big boy. He needed no adult supervision he would remind Granny.

Diamond loved to dance and sing anywhere. When she was ready to perform everything had to be removed from her stage; which often happened to be the dining room table. She knew it was a "no-no," so show time started as soon as Granny left the room and the coast was clear.

Sometimes while granny was cooking, Denzel and Diamond would get into all kinds of mischief. Jumping on Granny's bed, playing in her closet, knocking down her fancy dresses, and her church hats. Anything they could have fun with, nothing was off limits.

Denzel and Diamond did not like when it was almost time for Mom to leave for work. Denzel would often hide her keys and work I.D. badge in the freezer. He knew Mommy couldn't drive off without her keys or "clock in" without her work I.D. badge.

Together they would block the door smiling playfully, so Mommy would have to kiss them up to get by. Before she could say bye she had to distract them by sending them to get their favorite book or snack. Then she could slip out quickly and quietly without them pouting or looking sad.

They were too young to understand Mommy did not like leaving them at all. It made her sad too. At this time, she had no choice. Those were the hours she had to work.

If mommy did not go to work, they would not have all that yummy food, great books, and toys. Mommy's job allowed them to travel and live comfortably.

Many nights while at work, Mommy would pray for other ideas regarding choices of work that might allow her to spend more quality time with the children and Granny. She enjoyed her job helping people, but she could really use more sleep. She preferred to work in the daytime while they were still in school. That way she would be home to tuck them in bed, at night.

Mommy decided to go back to school and enhance her education. She felt this would allow her to have more control over the hours she worked.

This made the children very happy and Granny too. Now Granny could get more time to relax and Mommy would see more of Diamond's performances.

Now, when Denzel asked Mommy, "Do you work tonight?" She smiled and said, "No," I am staying home with my favorite boy; go get your favorite book so you can read me a story.

Since Mommy didn't have to work so many nights, the family was able to do their favorite things such as go to the beach and spend quality time.

Being a single mother was never my dream for us. God however, makes no mistakes. He does all things well. We have lived and we have learned together. Being your mom has taught me so much. I am grateful for you both. We are blessed! Denzel and Diamond, my prayer for you is that you soar higher than the eagles and follow all your dreams. Let God be your guide, there is nothing too hard for Him. To my parents thank you for your love and always guiding me to appreciate the value of reading. Much love to my supportive friends and family, I appreciate you. To every single parent, hold on and never give up. You have what it takes and you are not alone. Being a parent is never easy, but it has it's rewards. To every girl and every boy the sky is the limit, believe you can and you will!

Philippians 4:13

I can do ALL THINGS through Christ Jesus
who strengthens me.

Granny, my favorite girl, you have always been a figure of strength, and unconditional love in my life. Your actions have always expressed love without you speaking a word. You're dependable, strong and God fearing therefore I thank you for loving me in your own special way! I think of you often, especially when I say or do something you would do. I hope to be half the grandmother you have been to me!

Thank God for you!

Contact Leslie T. Marshall

www.leslietmarshall.com

Fountain of Life Publisher's House

www.pariceparker.biz